P9-DFT-789

OF LIFE AND OTHER SUCH MATTERS

BY
FELLA CEDERBAUM

Copyright © 2018 MahniVerse Press
All rights reserved
ISBN-10: 1983449687
ISBN-13: 978-1983449680

With greatest love and respect to my parents, whose horrific life experiences made me first reject, then question **everything** and finally embrace it all, as life unfolding on its own terms. I dedicate this book to Truth; to the Spark we all share.

There are only two ways to live your life. One is as though nothing is a miracle, the other is as though everything is a miracle.

-Albert Einstein

CONTENTS

Hush Those Tears **1**

Who Cries **3**

Rip The Bonds **5**

Glasses Of Your Reverie **7**

Of Causes And Conditions **11**

Some Kind of Shape **15**

I Sit And Wait **19**

A Test **23**

Scribbles on the Train **27**

Ropes **31**

Thud **33**

About Motivation And Intention **35**

Shofar **39**

In The Name Of Truth **45**

Truth **49**

Air **51**

What Makes You Cry **55**

Deeper Than Despair **59**

When Thoughts Stick To Your Mind **63**

Notes In The Sea **67**

I Dream Of You **71**

Wasted Hours **75**

Her Fancy Hairstyle **79**

Don't Look Around **83**

Those Very Movements **87**

It's Good For You **91**

Grief **97**

Meditation **99**

Hanging Inside **101**

Not Nothingness **105**

What We Know **109**

A Tear In My Heart **111**

Fear Or Excitement **113**

A Spark **117**

No Gyroscope **121**

Acknowledgements

PREFACE

The poems in this book constitute the first part of a series of over one hundred reflections that appeared spontaneously and unbidden over the span of four years. For most of my life I have questioned the nature of Truth, have pondered the way we construct meaning and reality, the nature of memory and what we refer to as mind, the location of which has so far eluded discovery. Questions about love, friendship, suffering, relationship, fear, death, grief, loneliness, religion, God and the origin of creativity led to a process of self-inquiry in the form of poetry.

My poetry reflections not only initiated themselves, but also emerged in the most unlikely circumstances of daily life. They were like an irresistible force that unerringly guided me to a place of greater, heart-felt understanding, frequently leaving me filled with gratitude, love and a new kind of happiness and peace.

In short, I have lived, loved, danced, searched and meditated. What I believed I could will into being has emerged on its own accord. Many years prior, spontaneous paintings had opened my creative doors to this journey, which has since taken me to the deepest reaches of inner space.

Repeated requests for a spoken version of the poems led to the creation of a series of short videos, incorporating some of my painting and set to my music. You can find them on **MahnoDahno.com**

Who is a whole man?
The one with a broken heart

-Rav Nachman of Bratislav

OF LIFE AND OTHER SUCH MATTERS

HUSH THOSE TEARS

October 2007, Train tracks leading to ashes in a black pit,
where thousands of bodies were burned

If I could stop my tears
I would stop them
Forever
If I could cry those tears
I would cry them
Forever
No tears
Neither not tears

Scorched arms
Reaching from the foul pit
Bodies transformed
Rugged rocks jutting
Petrified forever
And never there

Hush those tears
Remember!
Remember who you are
Not who you were
Remember who you are
Not now
Not then
But always and forever

Hush those tears
They are the ocean crying
And laughing

1

Laughing
And remembering
What was not forgotten

Laughing

Hush those tears
They are you
The clear light
Don't go
Don't stay
Remember!

Burned arms
Reaching into my heart
Tearing at my tears
Breaking what could not be broken

Could not
Can not
Neither there
Nor here
Neither now
Nor ever
Always here
And nowhere to be found

Scorched arms of clear light
Reaching

*****

WHO CRIES

October 18, 2011

I want to know
Who it is
Who cries
When the heart is overcome
With sweetness

Who cries
When recognition's dawn
Pervades my being?
Whose heart is it
That feels this sweetness?
And where does sweetness
The intoxicating bliss
Of everything
Where does it reside?

Who cries?
Whose heart?
Whose sweetness?
None of it mine
Yet all of it me

Who am I?
Who weeps with joy
And melts with love
That pours through everything that is?
True Nature?
Just a word
At bottom there is only
Bliss

RIP THE BONDS
November 1, 2011

Rip the bonds of therapeutic structures
Those labels cause the heart to fracture
Flee from the concepts
Of tiny vision
Of body parts and cell division
Flee to oblivion from those things
They just inflate all suffering

Fly free!
That is the motto now
Fly free!
And don't you ever bow
Don't even bow
To dedicated teachers
And don't hold wisdom's
Truest features

Don't hold Truth
That is not yours
Don't hold on
And don't endure
Throw out the words
But keep the teachings
And pay attention:
No more reaching
For attainments' glow
Or Realization
And give up
All your dedication

Now look closely
Can you see?

Exactly

Now
My Love
You are
Free

*****

GLASSES OF YOUR REVERIE

March 26, 2012

The Id is just another Me
Two kinds of egos plus Id makes three
A genius thought this up
To free
Those, who were trapped
And could not see
The truth that lay behind their suffering

I heard of this
Then tried it too
But there was nothing I could do
With all those concepts in my life
Which held much more than ego's plight
It held much tortured pain and bothers
Of ancestors, parents and all those others
Of all those others, who never spoke
And those, who thought it was a joke
That Jews were killed with such abandon
Could be forgotten
Life seemed random

Random killing
Random living
Random knowing
Of Awareness. Was it flowing
Through all those events
And all appearance?
Hence
I looked for a solution
Surpassing learned distribution

7

Of phrases all too finely crafted
To meditation I was drafted
To seek out Truth behind it all
Behind my thoughts and self
So tall
Behind notions about suffering
And comforts that are merely buffering
The impact of what is truly needed
To see the obvious
Unimpeded

See that everything is mere illusion
Like nightmare dreams come to conclusion
When you wake up and see quite clearly
How all ideas you hold so dearly
Whether dreaming or awake
Both are quite the same mistake

Both are intricate projections
On the mirror of perception
Just one glimpse behind its screen
Makes your recognize the dream

Now your journey can begin
And penetrate the constant din
Of everyday reality
And the sheer banality
Of what you hold with greatest force
Give it up!
Without remorse
Something new will bubble up
Life's expressions will not stop

Will continue for the sake
Of deepest Truth and throw its stake
Into the ground of everything
Until there is no more suffering

So you see? There's not one answer
To questions, such as "why this cancer?"
You cannot possibly hope to see
Through glasses of your reverie
Through dreamers' eyes that are half closed
Yet try to comprehend
Impose
Their inner views on outer worlds
Create huge theoretic swirls
Of how things are or why and what
Keeping you forever caught
In the web of explanations
Give them up
Those complications

Walk the Middle Way
Stay calm and firm
It will be easy to discern
What is true
How to proceed

That is really
All you need

*****

OF CAUSES AND CONDITIONS
March 26, 2012

What about causes and conditions?
What is fate and what is superstition?

It is like this, my friends
Look here
This apple is
It so appears
An independent growth event
But then
You'll find
It all depends

It came to be
There was a bee
There was a seed
Which had its course prescribed
Indeed

However, even if this truly was
The most perfect apple-cause
It could never quite develop
Unless it had earth
Not yellow
Nor parched, nor dry, nor soggy
And sun that shone through clouds
When foggy
And neither storms, nor hail
Nor birds
That ate the thing before full girth

But once the full-grown fruit appears
will you investigate arrears
Of all of those conditions past?
Your mind forgets them very fast

Right here, there is another matter:
Where did the seed come from
Or better:
How is it seeds before that grew?
And then before the first you knew?
My point is that there is no way
Unless omniscient
You can say:
This is the cause, hence that some karma
Since, notwithstanding lofty thought
You surely know but almost naught
Of all that might have given rise
You can, at best, surmise
What happened here, or there, or ever
While you feel you are so clever
Because in your deluded ways
You make up stories and then say:
"This is what made that happen"
Right?

Sheer ignorance with all its might
Will bring its very own correction
Of minds' erroneous inflections
Until your deepest lies subside
Compelling you to never hide
Not from the Truth, nor from yourself
Nor behind sayings on your shelf

Allowing none but the essential
Not worshipping the accidental
Cleverly constructed universes
Which your mind holds and rehearses
With great abandon and delight
Laying to waste
Its truest might

So I tell you
Don't get distracted
By your eyes' conclusions
Nor by your perceptual delusions
Eat the apple
But know its nature
As its most essential feature
Look through your eyes
And through their vision
And notice that there's no division
Between the seer and the seen
Between the causes and the gleam
In everything you can behold
There're no exceptions
Be fierce and bold!
Drop those ideas you really cherish
Let your mind dance like a dervish
Calling for complete surrender
See?
Your heart will jump
And you?
Are
Free

*****

SOME KIND OF SHAPE

April 8, 2012

I hear something:
It has a shape of some kind
It is not as like listening
To a rambling mind
It is more like a baby
That wants to be born
It hovers in space
And feels rather forlorn
I open the door
And allow it to land
And say what it needs
While moving my hand

I move my hand
And the words stream out
Yet when it starts gives no clue
What it might be about

So I scribble away
Whenever it calls
Sometimes while driving
Or in shower stall
I scribble fast to get it all down
Am curious about it
Yet never frown
Have no expectations
So it's free to express
To go where it wishes
I must confess
That I love what it's doing

15

Can tell it is true
And so wish it is helpful
Spiritually too

I will sit and wait
And hear what it wants
It appears
That I found a truth without taunts
Not a talent or something
Inherently agonizing
With manifestations
Reluctant or cauterizing

What is it
I ask
Yet dare not know
Just in case it will stop
Its magnificent flow
Its stream so delicious
Unbounded and free
Unerringly holds me
Until I can see
The place
Where it wanted to go all along
And all I do
Is to write down its song

It feels that a confluence
Of all I have learned
Have studied and read
And searched and yearned
Is now taking shape

From a different me
One that has dropped
The constructions we see
I am still her
Yet don't care exactly the same
In fact
It's an entirely different game

Hmmm

Still not the answer, or deepest truth
Why this is happening in age
Not in youth
Well, to be honest
I just know the "how"
Of that place in me
That seems to allow
Expecting nothing
Except
For that dot
Of moment's expression
Then goes in the pot

The pot of exuberance of all there is
The light and the total darkness
Of bliss

*****

I SIT AND WAIT
April 8, 2012

I had a boyfriend, a musician
He could compose like a magician
I asked him:
What is it you do?
How do you write an instant Blues?
How are your chords magnificent
Before your even know the end?
Before composition's conclusion
You already pierced occlusion
Of that, which normally blocks the way
And holds most artists right at bay
From arriving where they aim
Writer's block it's often named

What is it you do? I ask
Can you help me tear the mask?
The mask that's holding in True Face
Of what exists in inner space?

He said:
I just sit down
And wait
At the piano I just stay
I sit and wait. That's all I do
The rest, I trust, will just come through

I take my hands off both my knees
And place my fingers on the keys
They start to play all that I hear
It is not coming from my ear

I see the notes, dancing in space
They gently blow across my face
They coax my fingers
To express
They must have found the right address

Then I keep playing this and that
Repeat a phrase
But never cut
Or edit things before their time
So all the notes have equal shine
Until the moment, when it's clear
There is a song that has appeared
A song, a symphony or dirge
They all appear with equal urge
It might be any other form
All are welcomed
There is no norm
The only rule there is for me
That what I write it totally free

What I write comes as a gift
From the Divine
Comes to uplift
Our life of suffering on this earth
To balance out our human birth
That leads to hardship by default
So music is creation's call
To remember what is true
Behind imagined me and you
Behind the density of being
That hides the sound of inner seeing

Music reminds us who we are
When we get lost in
What's too far
From the truth of everything
And from the song
Your heart can sing

Let music's magic
Steal your soul
Let your rhythm
Follow it's call

Its Truth
Quite ineradicable
Will lead beyond
The unimaginable

Whichever path
It beckons your plot

Fathomable
It is not

*****

A TEST

April 8, 2012, Late Night

Did you know this is a test?
To find out, who endures the best?
To check hardiness in the face
Of suffering, violence and race
Of killing, torture, hunger, pain
And fear of nothing left to gain
Of knowing nothing beyond vanity
Or being born in need of charity
Of being raised in ignorance
Or never having one small chance
Of ever making it in life
From birth to death
Nothing
But strife

Did you know this is a test?
To find out, who endures the best?
Endures
Yet looking for the answers
That lie beyond all human cancers?
Answers beyond the constant stress
Of lives that are a holy mess
To learn disaster, mess and all
Are merely trap-doors
Make you fall
Hopefully into abyss
With not a penny's worth of bliss
With nothing, but fecundest darkness
Its moisture far beyond mere starkness
Relentlessness the fertile ground

23

For all that is to be unbound
Unbound from mere interpretations
Unbound from thinking, ideations
Freed from its very substance too
Till nothing left to hold wrong view

Did you know this was a test
To guide you to endure the rest?
Demands to look with naked eyes
At all phenomena that rise
Or, actually, appear to rise
Which is
When to your great surprise
You recognize that
Which you've always known:
True Nature
Both, as silence and as tone
Both, as sufferer and suffering
As well as worshipper and offering
We see that doer and the deed
And the result
Are just one seed
Of momentary preference
Of action versus deference

It was a test of mind and heart
A test!
A call, to make you smart
Invitation of Compassion
To bring you home, in its own fashion
Hard to recognize at first
Unless born with unquenched thirst

To drink nectar of the One Truth
That's why
It is mostly not in youth
You finally get to taste from it
Which is, why suffering exists

Persists to bring you safely home
Not wasting life-times
Where you roam
Through universes of desire
Or those of greed and hate
It would mire
This truest of endeavors
So this suffering is quite clever

It is instrument, path and test
All One
Until you are truly, truly done
Done!
When True Nature is revealed
From endless layers of thoughts unpeeled
Unveiled from mind-obstructing views
And great delusions in the stew

Did you know you passed the test?
When you surrendered and let your mind rest?
When Awareness rests itself
Expresses
And spontaneously progresses
To be still, unchanged forever
You are
Free

And can be clever
It is important how you meet
Each instance laid down at your feet
Each instance
Now the same to you
No longer matters what you do
What matters is right motivation
Without the slightest deviation

Not right, nor left, nor anywhere
Will help transcend the test
Take care
It's only, when you look within
And go beyond your every whim
Of thinking you can conquer this
No hiding behind lazy bliss!

So endurance was the test
While you searched and held your breath
Now go home
You know the path
It leads straight
To your own
Heart

*****

SCRIBBLES ON THE TRAIN
June 4, 2012

Do you know how accomplished you are?
You beat out millions of sperms so far
You were not even in the world yet to know
Competition, or rat race or honours bestowed

Do you know how amazing you really are?
You survived countless deaths
You are a star
You have been mother and father and child to all
You've heard gods and demons
And followed their call
You have been wealthy, sick, poor and destitute too
You have been Christian, Buddhist, Hindu and Jew

You have mourned endless deaths
Buried many a son
You have been shaman, hermit, monk, rabbi and nun
You have been a king and a beggar
Asking alms to survive
You have waited for saviors that never arrived
You have tortured and thought
You were not to be blamed
You starved, drowned, hung
Have been burned and maimed

Your atoms have cycled for eons untold
You have been iron, palladium, copper, silver and gold
You have been earth, ether, fire and the ocean of all
Yet, you are none of the things with a name to call

27

So now I ask you the question again:
Do you know
You are accomplished?
A leader of men?
Can you see?
You are accomplished beyond many a dream
Just look with the eyes
Of the Clear Light gleam

It's for you to remember True Nature
Right Now
And give all your doubts a courteous bow
That bow bids farewell to all that's not you
And to all you have attached to whatever you do
Just look with the light that I see in your eyes
What you will find will be new
Yet no great surprise

You have known all along
How accomplished you are
It was clear in your heart
That nothing could mar
The Truth you have held
And pursued all your life
Now go
Lay down what is left of your strife
You have moved
Through the thick and the thin of creation
So now you can be
And live with elation

Continue to see
Through the eyes of compassion
Pursue waking up with your greatest passion
There is nothing to hold a torch to the Truth
There is nothing better for our future youth

As your being shines forth
Great Love will abound
You will leave no more traces in
In the infinite ground

You are infinite, endless, unbound and free
You are the tiniest fragment of creative glee
You are all and nothing
So remember:
No Doubt
You will inhabit forever what this is about
It is timeless
I know this
But don't ask me how
See you next time, my friends
This is all for now

*****

ROPES

June 8, 2012

By which rope
Will you hang yourself this life?
I ask you
Do you know?

I ask, because we mostly think
That it is fate alone that deals us blows
Isn't that so?

We think that life just hands us
Random burdens we must muster
Don't you agree?
But I am beginning to decipher a pattern
To events that lose their luster
Do you see?

I have heard rumours about learning lessons
And repeating them
That's quite a drag

Have you noticed, when you pay attention?
Look beyond your personal mayhem?
That's the snag

There are billions just like you
All have a rope
Hang by their navel
Then come out
Forget the scope
That's where it starts

Think they are one, because of their umbilicus
Forget those billions
With same homunculus
Time to get smart

Think with you heart and see the rope
Uniquely tailored just for you
Don't give up hope
You get my drift?

Those ropes are tailored for us mortals
Hang us only, if we try to duck
Try to elope their portals
How ever swift

I want to hear those secrets
Sound out loud
For you, my friend
For you, my love
That is all this is about

*****

THUD

August 4, 2012, 3AM, Israel

When they throw me with a thud
And they cover me with mud
I want to witness
All awakened
Know the light

When my earthly sorrows end
And I've made all my amends
I want to know
That I have passed
This test of life

Passed the test of loving well
Of transcending every hell
That I created
Or may have caused
By lazy bliss

Want to leave without a trace
Knowing me in every face
Only one
There is to know
With not one miss

When I laid down on my grave
There was nothing left to save
Except for shining dots
That lead
To the Unbound

I imagined how it feels
To be bodiless and peeled
Naked inside
Wrapped in shroud
And not a sound

Before I sail, right on the helm
Of the unembodied realm
And cross rivers
Of rememb'ring
What is true

So right now, by facing death
Truth is absolute
No less
I will stay on course
And practice
Till I'm blue

Truest blue is what I meant
Yet, in fact, it's not the end
But I need more time
To understand
The course

Of the path that is prescribed
In my deepest heart inscribed
Follow shining dots
Then leave
Without remorse

*****

ABOUT MOTIVATION AND INTENTION
September 8, 2012

Motivation and Intention are not
As you might think, identical
One is driving force, to underlying goal
Which sometimes might appear
Quite frantical
The other is so very sneaky
Like a great actor, posturing
As that, which sounds amazing
But serves selfish prospering

Intention might be pure and lofty
Camouflaging very softly
What is truly motivating
Merely self-enhancing
Stating
One thing as the cause for action
When, below the surface
Suction
Of desire drives
Often of considerable size

No ill wish may be in wait
But that can never quite negate
Truth of a, sadly, lowly riff
That serves the self, especially if
It presents itself with righteous smile
Eyes, downcast, with perfect style:

Look here

It's me again
So noble
Please look at all my qualities
In total
Look at all the things I do
Can you see?
I have the view

So now I have a single question:
Do you think it's true intention?
Or have you noticed some dismay?
Seen that it has gone astray?
Held in the grip of some delusion
Not aware of Truth's occlusion?

However in your mind you hold
Some thoughts of pure intention?
Bold
Intention, now reduced to concept
Motivation deftly sidestepped
The conditions for release
Of karmic traces
They won't cease
Nor stop forming
They'll start storming

And you are back
In thought constructions
That held you hostage
It's destruction
Of your path

You dithered!
What a case of
Truth quite withered
In Buddhist terms:
Your path so far
A certain case of
Ma-Rigpa

*****

SHOFAR

Rosh Hashanah 2012

When I heard the Shofar
I cried sweet tears
And could not stop their flow
Had no idea what moved inside me
Deeply set aglow
My *neshama* with its yearning
To be one and not forget
What is written
In my deepest heart
In rays of light it's set

Rays of light
That shine with nothing
But the only Truth there is
Rays of light
That are the substance
And the message not to miss
It is the message
Of remembering
Is it not?

You might ask
What to remember
And then leave
Before you know
Do you think
You can afford to drop the ball
And let it go?
Is that true?

It is your destiny that is ringing
When the Shofar's wailing sound
Calls to permeate
To penetrate your bones
Until you are found
That's the cue

When all thinking
Has surrendered
And your ego follows suit
You will find
That there is something
That is sweeter than pursuit
Of activities of living
In success and failure's realm
You will find
That other something
That just never needs a balm
That is a fact

So I heard the Shofar
Singing to my soul
From other times
And its wailing and resounding
Propelled my heart
To climb and climb
With the deepest love
Of everything inhabiting my life
Even pain and fear and suffering
And my very recent strife
Made a pact

Made a pact of great significance
It changed my life forever
There was nothing in my offering
That allowed for it to sever
So I am here to witness all of it
And know these tears are true

Because they bear the light
Of all there is
That only Truth imbues
Light that sees

Light with eyes, ears
And omniscience
Light that cannot ever end
Light in darkness
Through all heavens
And all hells
It transcends
No beginning and no ending
To delineate or call
Defying names and concepts
Which are dear, yet make us fall
That is peace

It is peace beyond serenity
That follows wars and fights
But this peace
Lies in the very things
You oppose with all your might
It is the stillness
That is everywhere

You find your life is turning
It accompanies the very things
That trigger all your yearnings
It resides inside the loudest sound
And in the softest whisper
It remains unchanged
And undeceived
By temptations of the scripture

The Shofar's sound
Its closest twin
They are different, but the same
The only difference I know
Lies merely in the name
But names are tricky
From the start
They lead us far astray
When nameless Truth
Is here for us
Unwavering
Shows us the way

Shows us the way
To stay on track
And not forget to ask
The question that's forever here
And is our foremost task
The question that's the only one
The only one with meaning
So now I ask you:
Do you know your task?
Let us start and do the cleaning

The cleaning of perception's lens
The cleaning of our heart
Yom Kippur's Shofar will do the rest
And offer a new start

It's all right here
Immediate to the eye
An instant recognition's spark
All suffering defies

*****

IN THE NAME OF TRUTH
October 29, 2012

I am finally done
Done with teachers
Who torch their students' heart
In the name of Truth
They say

I am done with Truth
That is less
Than love's compassion
And done with kind hearts
That break the other
In the name of Truth
They say

I am done with drunken delirium
That professes the wisdom
It claims to protect
And done with teachers
Who show off what they know
And teach what they don't
In the name of Truth
They say

I am done with self-filled anger
That hails from skin
Not from the heart of wisdom
Nor from the heart of compassion
And done with teachings
That spring from the mind
Because arrogant hearts
Made vision blind

45

I am done with believing
Deluded perceptions
Rather than what my heart dictates
Dictated from the beginning of time
Eternal and always
In the name of Truth
I say

I am done with being chosen
By those who have no right to choose
Until their choosing
Springs from Truth
The one inevitable truth
Of who we are

Of who we are
Beginningless and forever after

The one Truth
The one Heart
Pervading all that is
All that was
And all there can ever be
One Truth
One Love
One Heart
One Love
Neither rejecting
Nor proclaiming
Anything it knows

As other than itself

I am done with all
That does not taste like the bell
Of crystalline light
Inside my mouth
And permeates my being
With the sweetness
Of despair and love
Infused as one
I am done with all of that
In the name of Truth
I say

In the name of Truth
I will cherish that
Which cannot be uncherished
Cannot be mistaken
When seen with naked eyes
In the name of Truth
I will pierce the light
That cannot be extinguished
I will hold its flame
And let it burn my soul
Let it burn my soul with love
That has no name

No name to call its own
The only love there is

In the name of Truth
I say

*****

47

TRUTH
November 20, 2012

Do you know what Truth is?
I don't
I thought I knew
And then it turned on its head
And I?
I danced on my ear

Do you know what Truth is?
I don't
I was looking for it
And then it wandered away
It wandered into the distance
And I?
I swung on my eye

Do you know what Truth is?
I don't
I recognize it
But I don't know what it is
I thought I did
But then it turned inside out
And I?
I hopped on my hair

Have you ever danced on your ear
When Truth was there
And then it was not?
Have you swung on your eye
When you touched Truth

And your hand
Reached through a cloud?
Have you hopped on your
When Truth was black
And then it was white?

How is it that Truth
Is nowhere to be found?
I mean, nowhere to be found
But then it permeates all
Permeates your most desperate heart
And your darkest night?

How is it that Truth is invisible
When you crane your neck
For a whiff of its fragrance
Just when you fade into its dream?

Do you know what Truth is?

*****

AIR

December 10, 2012

I looked at what remains
When all is but impermanent
What's left?
I asked and searched
Beyond the mere establishment
Of concepts, words, descriptions
And such things
When what I yearned to find
Was far beyond those offerings

Is there nothing
To fill that thoughtless void?
Is it air?
Or a decoy?

She said:
Describe to me what's air
And I pondered
And wondered what it was
Or was that splitting hairs?
Is air described
By what it's clearly **not**?
Yet by everything?
All?
Down to the tiniest dot?

We don't see air
Yet it is clearly present
It suffuses most the things
That lie in earth and heaven

Almost nothing lives without it
Yet alone
It is not sufficient

Well
Air is not
But Awareness is omniscient
It is what creates
As out of very air
All manifestations

Those that tear
The heart
Or bathe us in its sweetness
Or those of strength
Or sheer and utter
Meekness

This air
That puzzled me so strangely
Is not like Consciousness
Because mainly
It too springs forth
From the one source
It too is empty
Even while with greatest force
It blows through oceans
Lives and atmospheres
Just when it thickens
Right before it disappears

So what is air?

Could that still be the question
Or should we ponder what is left
Beyond our asking bastion?
What is left when all is empty
Way before its mention?

And what is left
When Truth shines forth
With magnificent intention?
We find that just like air
It is ubiquitous
But loves in all directions
With not a trace restrictiveness
It is the reason
Why we ask our questions
Suffer pain
It is the driving force
Of every single search in vain

Now do you know
Why air caused such a muddle?
Do you see how fast
It makes us all befuddled?
In just one instance
Of negating all
We find that air has taken us
For yet another fall

It's what created air
We have been looking for
We will continue doing so
Way beyond death's door

Until it's clear
And never to be lost

That losing sight of it
Can have a heavy cost

So cleave to it, my friends
And continue with your practice
And pay attention where you are
Along this central axis
Of the eternal
Versus nihilism's route

One liberates

The other?
Leaves a constant pout

*****

WHAT MAKES YOU CRY

December 11, 2012

I know what makes you cry
When listening to my words
Of air, awareness and of things
That we have often heard
It seems you cry
When you feel I listen

I do listen
But something else is kissing
The lining of your yearning heart
Reminding you of sweetness
Your own
From way before your very start

I hear a question. but then I travel far
Into a deeper realm
And find the door ajar
I open it
And listened to the music
Whispering
Stroking my soul
Caressing wounded festering

Out stream the words
That tell me what is true
Out comes the Truth I know
Inside of me and you
So when you hear my words
Clearly express
The things you know

55

There is a pain in you
Quite deep, yet in the flow
An ancient pain
Of love and generosity
An ache, a burning
Far from religiosity
It comes from longing
That I too know well
It springs from seeking
From having much to tell

You are telling it, my friend
In all your endless ways
At home, in work and offerings
Spectacular display
So we share words and tears
And laughs and ancient fears
I feel so touched by that
Beyond how it appears

I am so moved
By being deeply known
My whisperings to be heard
Before they are intoned
It is so precious to reciprocate
That which when absent
So often will deflate
Assurance of the deepest kind
Assurance
Of the one great mind

The one great mind

The sphere of everything
Yet never bound by thoughts
Or our constructed things

The one great mind
Creating all there is
Our hearts, our words
And all our earthly bliss
Our tears
The moisture of a living heart
Full of compassionate presence
For all and every part

Its flowering
Magnificent in bloom
Of wisdom
Even in the greatest doom
A wisdom deep
Encompassing and sweet
That's where, my friend
We will forever meet
Forever since the timeless dot
Before beginning
Endless
Compassionate and hot

Hot with the burning
Of creative glee
Bursting through all there is
Just wait and see
If you have any doubt
That this is true

That's all for now
We're all moving into blue
Into the blue of all
That can be known
And not
And even further
Than the farthest dot
On the horizon of this universe
Which is the spark
That drove this verse

*****

DEEPER THAN DESPAIR

December 11, 2012

I have known a dread in me
That is deeper than despair
It cuts through everything I know
And feels like a huge tear
Right through the fabric
Of my favourite constructions
The ones I hold most dearly
Held by deep seduction

Seduction of my thoughts
That say they'll think it through
Seduction of my heart, believing
That it is totally true
That there is logic
In this endless universe
That there is reason
Why some lives appear
Quite simply cursed

Cursed to the naked eye
Yet little do you truly know
Of causes and conditions
That deal such mighty blows
Just like the best of us
Can hardly ever figure
Why love appears
Right when you cross the river

The river of remembering
Who you truly are

59

And not of how you have succeeded
In conquering life so far

So is this dread simply another cloud?
A mere obstruction
With no further clout?
A mere result of mind habituation
That lead astray from Truth
And the impending liberation?

I have an inkling
That everything can change
The moment quite precise
When within shooting range
You look a challenge
Right into the eye
Then deconstruct it
Let it truly fly

But then what happens
Is the strangest thing
That which oppressed you
Is now liberation's wing
It takes you soaring
Further than you ever ventured
You'll find the bonds of pain
Quite severed
Morphed into adventure
Of instant after instant
Of profound expression
Eternally surprising you
With lesson upon lesson

Which, when encountered
With compassion
And surrender
Are quite delicious
Even when so tender
You think that one more thing
Is more than you can suffer
Then recognize the Truth
Your life just proffered

The Truth that's always
Right within your view
Just sometimes clouded
By not staying true
Not cleaving to it
The way you had intended
But soon enough
That too will be upended

So cling to nothing
Allow all to unfold
Exuberant and lively
Just as you have been told
By what you know
From deep inside your heart
So bottom line:
Don't run and dart
Around in circles
Chasing your own tail
When all you need is here
Just hoist the proper sail
You know exactly
What I mean by that

But here it is:

Don't be a lazy cat
Don't rest your mind and fall asleep
But rest right where
Awakening is deep
Where what remains
Is bright and true
And where there's only
One True Nature:
You

*****

WHEN THOUGHTS
STICK TO YOUR MIND

February 8, 2013

Do you know who you are
When thoughts stick to your mind?
Do you know who you are
When despair makes you blind?
Do you know what is right
When your ailments alight
And your longing is all that remains?

Have you known utter joy
And then felt like a toy
In the hands of a God quite amused?
Have you dreamt you could fly
And then eons went by
Yet your wings stayed untouched
And unused?

Have you yearned to be taught
And then found life was fraught
With delusions so grand that you ran?
Have you trusted a friend
Who then failed to amend
What turned out to be all but a sham?

Have your tears ever seemed
like an unending stream
In a loneliness
Vast
Just like space?

And a sweetness ensued
That completely imbued
Cloaked your heart, mind and soul
With its grace?

Do you know what I mean
When I say I still dream
To wake up from this life and be free?
Do you think it is mad
That life can be so sad
Yet your heart can be strong
Like a tree?

Can you remember a time
When life seemed sublime
And a fear rose
From nowhere you knew?
There was nothing but fear
While your mind disappeared
Yet a knowing of more rose in you?

When this knowing matured
Through the suffering endured
And a shining suffused all there is?
When this tempering of steel
Strengthened heart, soul and heel
And your pain
Is transformed into bliss?

Do you know how it feels
When Compassion unpeels
All the layers of doubt that can mar?

When your heart gets so wide
That all beings abide
Inside you
And there's space for the stars?

For the stars to light up
For the darkness to drop
As your light shines through all?
It is true!
Do you know what I mean
When I say it's a dream?
Let's wake up and know Love is the glue

Is the glue of creation
Of each atom or nation
That is all
There is nothing to do

*****

NOTES IN THE SEA

February 9, 2013

So
I have been wondering who I am
And where I was before this life began
Wondering who I am in this entire thing
Which note in the sea of suffering
And which voice in the symphony of life
And what beat
Which rhythm makes us fight
What is the sound of our deepest voice?
Which note rings out beyond the noise
Of merely living day by day
And then noticing with dismay
How the very fabric of this world
Disintegrates and just unfurls
Its deepest rumblings
Grand
Beyond imagination
While dancing waves
Resound with liberation

The note of "I" is now the song of us
The name we yearned
Not worth the slightest fuss
Of seeking out its origin or nature
Rather than knowing
That its truest feature
Is that it holds the key to all
So listen well and heed its magic call
Ignore the warnings you have heard
Reclaim your freedom

Like a bird
Spread wings and fly with great abandon
Resist temptation to think
That Paris, Rome or London
Are destinations for your perfect flight
There is one great journey
We all must take
Right?

Just go beyond the furthest destination
Way further than imaginations
Then look
Beyond the very end
Of everything you comprehend
And then?
Beyond mere comprehending
Though you might think
It's never-ending
That's right!
There is always more to come
Yet then
One day
You will find you are absolutely done

You will be done, eliminating this or that
You will not find a head to put your hat
You will not find me talking, either
There won't be both of us
Nor neither

And if you think
This will take lifetimes to complete

Since path to wisdom is no easy feat
You are wrong again
Because all that is required

Is for you not to get mired
In what you think you should be doing

It is not doing, but quite simply shooing
The flimsy tatters of a mind obstructed
And then behold what is true
That's all!
It is not protracted
Nor is it complicated in the least
It is more like going to a feast
And recognizing that the food and wine
Just in themselves are not Divine

It is Divinity in all
Which, when we miss
Is our greatest fall
Our fall into the trap of ignorance
Right back into delusion's dance

Now please remember:
No regrets
For having taken some wrong steps
All steps are right, no matter what you do
When you remember, what is always true
Is true in happiness and in the worst of hells
Even when you cannot tell
That liberation is right here for you
Just trust me
This is more than true

*****

I DREAM OF YOU
March 1, 2013

Whenever I dream of you
You seem to be obscured
I cannot see your face
But I know it to be pure
You appear to me
And clearly have a message
Can you tell me what it is?
Where is the hidden passage?

I don't know you
But you fill my dreams
And my heart jumps
And bursts its very seams
Our connection is immense
Your presence
Beyond wondrous and intense
My quest to merge
So strong and fierce
Burning
My eyes a well of tears
The time has come
Escape
Take off and fly
To realms much wider than the sky

Wider than skies beyond all space
Wider than all creation behind my face
Behind the face that I have called my own
Though it is nothing but a slight misnome

The truth is that your face
Exactly as your dreams
Is nothing other than some shining gleam

Of that which is true
When you love
From deep within and from way above
When you love all that is
When all that is
Expressed
When there is nowhere to go
Nor to ask what might be next

What comes next has been here for eons
Forever
Now is the moment
The true endeavour
Of living while dying
And bearing our pain
There is nothing else
There is nothing to gain

Do not look elsewhere
Nor dig deep inside
But take every instant
In an even stride
Embrace this moment
And the next
And the next
That is all you will read
In the best of texts
You will find it in sutras

Bibles, legends
And in tales
That True Nature, when found
Makes all you know just pale

Pale in dimension and scope
And expression
Simply watch the unending succession
Of everything
Bursting
Exploding with light
Simply remember with all of your might
That which is you
And has always been

Exactly the way I started this dream

*****

WASTED HOURS
April 16, 2013, Train to Penn

Did this trip turn out much longer
Than you could ever fathom?
More than unpredictable
And heavy to bear in your bosom?
How could you know life
Before you had tasted
How could you appreciate
Precious hours just wasted

Only you know
Which moments flew by unattended
It is you who must look
Without feeling offended
Look at moments you allowed
To melt into space
Just like clouds that thin out
And show sky's blue face

Now I ask you
Before you grieve unending losses
I ask you
Before you are covered by mosses
Do you want all these things
That behave like those clouds
Or is it the sky that this is about?
Is it time that has vanished
Is gone?
Or is Awareness that
Which allowed it to roam?

It is Awareness itself
That can never be wasted
Even while Alice's rabbit is

Late
Late
Late
And hasted

So you are right here
Nothing gone, nothing left
Even while ageing
An outrageous theft
Of all that you held
As the things most dear
Until one day
It became blatantly clear
That all that, which you named
With abandon
And inhabited deeply
Was actually random
In terms of the deeply unfolding
Expression
Quite unnamable
By our living obsessions

You can neither avoid it
Nor ignore
Nor desire
It is a timeless, unbounded
Unceasing fire

The burning of sparks united as one
So don't sit on your laurels

And think you are done
When a light or some bliss
Make one splendid appearance
Conceptualizations!
Like you, me
And all heavenly clearance

Mere thought combinations!
Named
Invented by mind
While the Truth you are seeking
Ended up
Left behind
Left behind like a diamond
Undetected
Because black
Not discovered
While your path went astray
And quite off-track

So come back and remember
What you know in your bones
What you've known from the moment
Your being had honed
Its intention to wake up
And then fly
Now rest still
And contented
And no time goes by

*****

HER FANCY HAIRSTYLE

April 18, 2013, Train to Penn. Again

He said: "You are a mystic"
I heard:
"A mistake?"
He said:
"No! A mystic"
And I thought:
"Is he serious?"
As my mood went from sad
To almost delirious

I get off the train and a woman informs me with great
intensity:
"The woman had a fancy HAIRSTYLE. THAT is why I
got thrown out of a restaurant ...... because she had a
fancy hairstyle!"
"Wow" I say
"I went in and asked for a soup and they overCHARGED
me! She said it was $6. SIX DOLLARS for a PINT of
soup. It should have been $5! They overcharged me!"
"THAT was unfair" I say
"Yes, it WAS. So I drank the water and she THREW ME
OUT!"
"Wow" I say.
"Yes! That's what she did ......because she had a fancy
HAIRSTYLE!"

So where was I
When I pondered the mistake of me
And how such a tiny word
Can sting like a bee

And destroy most of the notions
We carry around
Of death and meaning
And answers not found
While the next word
Can float you right into space
As though you had grown
A brand new face

But what about hairstyles?
And fancy ones yet?
Have you considered that meaning?
You didn't
I bet
Didn't' you wonder
How words can be scrambled
In any odd fashion?
Then you make up stories with greatest passion
Like that lady saw a hairstyle so fancy and off
Then drank the water
While the waitress scoffed
I have to tell you
It was that hairstyle that did it
It is getting clearer from minute to minute

The guy on the next train has another story
Loudly he tells of "the others"
The scenario sounds gory
It is obviously true, but I hear in his voice
That in desperate manner
He feels without choice
No choice how to be in the life he is living

A life where he never experienced giving
Or rather
Being given some love
By anyone close
Or from above

From above that is distant
And not of his world
He talks of sewers, damage
And unfairness unfurled
I hear f….ing this and damn that
And I forget
The mistake
So that is what happens
When perceptions are fake
Or real
Or just in-between
They all lose their luster
In an ongoing stream
Of events moving
This way or that
And off we go
To the realm of
Tit for tat

He said this and I thought
What?
Great conversation it is certainly not
I had felt sadness, yet then it was gone
And he?
Never knew even part of this song

Your stories are endless and so are reactions
That keep you suspended in constant traction

Which crazy lady or what deranged thought
Will be next on your menu that is densely fraught
With traps and dead-ends that lead you astray
So remember to throw the menu away
Fling it out
But partake in the feast
Of experienced instants
Then feed all to the beasts
Of forgetting
So the remnants don't stick
And your heart remains
Without even the slightest nick

It will open itself to something enormous
So huge
Radiantly stainless in a shining deluge

Neither thoughts nor feelings
Can possibly sever
This locationless space that is you
Forever
Forever, eternal
Beyond space and time
Beyond mistakes, mystics
Or what you call dirt
Or
Sublime

*****

DONT LOOK AROUND
April 25, 2013

Don't look around
Don't try to gage
What might be people's strange reactions
They all come with their own contractions
Fear of silence
Fear of thoughts
Fear of nothing
Fears they ought
To have
Because they are told
Some things are just not done
When you are old

Nor are they done
When you are a young thing
Nor at some other age
Just in-between
In other words, there is no time
To be true to yourself
Just whine
That life is sad
The news is bad
Terrorists are on the prowl
And the weather is unusually foul

What else is new?
You pay your dues this time around
And maybe next time you rebound
In a body without karmic traces
So all you'll leave behind?

Shoe-laces!
Not hair, nor nails
As you have been told
That is because
If not bold
You have no idea of ancient times
In this culture
Not too sublime
We leave behind something quite trivial
Hoping to make the next life convivial

The point is
Stop procrastinating
With all that is oh, so fascinating
Those diversions, merely obscuring
While you are constantly procuring
The one thing
Then just one thing more

Where is your attention to the core
Of what is driving your old engine?
It is much simpler than you can imagine
The answer is here
Has always been
See?
You knew it
I can tell by the gleam
That lights your eyes in recognition
Now your path can reach fruition
When your deeds are pure expression
Far beyond some glamorous professions
Or the things you deemed so central

Whether physical or mental
The essential will emerge
Show up with ever greater urge
Will guide you
Push you without ceasing
While non-essentials are releasing
Their grip on what you called your life

You see?

Now?

You are alive

*****

THOSE VERY MOVEMENTS
April 26, 2013, Harold's Concert

Bursting forth, controlled
Yet wild
Are those very movements
Which
When a child
You learn to hold in
Tightly grasped
Below the view of who might ask
About that stirring in your soul
But really stirring
Whirling
Without goal
Without a purpose
Other than itself
Complete abandon
Dancing elf of whispers, bellows
Screams and songs
Of endless notes
None of them wrong
None of them right
Every one of them
With its own light
A symphony of being
Of vibrant colours beyond seeing
A symphony of all a life can hold
And when expressed is not called
Bold
Since everything is bold
As long as true
As long as it is all of you

Is all of you
And then some more
It is what opens up the door
To that
Which you have searched outside
Of things that took you on the ride
Through the fabric of your life
Of your existence cut by a knife
Or feather
Or a word
So harsh
Or kind
Those things that make your senses blind

While blinded
You begin to really see
How secrets hide themselves with glee
Right inside the inner you
Your spark
That will not shine on queue

Yet its piercing gleam was always here
And that is, what gives rise to fear
It is so close that we forget
There simply is no need to fret
Nor search
Nor run here and thither
But remember
Better not to dither
Just move in one straight line of heart
Keep your intention never far apart

And your motivation quite unchanged
That is how the Universe arranged
For you to recognize what's wise
And penetrate unspoken lies

Now
Recognize truth by ignoring
All thoughts that are too wise
Or boring
Far from true goal in this existence
So stay on track
With great persistence
Even while life may taste quite tart
Don't give up
And trust your heart

*****

ITS GOOD FOR YOU

May 5, 2013

Have you ever asked yourself why bother at all
With therapy, drugs, or interventions so tall
That the cure is much worse than the illness at hand
Once you found that you landed in doctor-land?
Eat a healthy breakfast
Don't do this, nor do that
Exercise more
Eat well
Don't get fat

Have you ever thought that maybe it is better
Not to follow instructions quite to the letter?
Have you ever considered setting up your own rules
And defend them stubbornly just like a mule?

In any case
I did have some thoughts in this matter
Especially after events almost shattered
The remnants of trust in experts' opinions
As though our bodies are their dominion
With so-called facts ever changing
I will make a sure choice
I will put it in writing
This is my voice

When I will be told that the time has come
That my days are numbered
And it's my turn to go home
Cadbury Milk Chocolate
Will be the first thing I eat

91

In fact, I will eat it
As much as I please
For breakfast and lunch
For snacks and for dinner
With neither the slightest notion
Nor shimmer
Of concern or worry
About calories or dairy
Or toxins
No
I will dance and be merry
And ride on the wings of sheer indulging

On those wings we all learn to reign in
To stop bulging
In all the wrong places
Then pack on some weight
Who cares how we look
When we arrive at the gate

I will know my True Nature
A big smile on my face
With that Cadbury smile
Which has been missing of late
It somehow got lost
In the midst of my search
Leaving me tired on a dreamless perch

Yet for now I will go back
To a healthy routine
Starting my day with a breakfast
So clean

So healthy
That my intestines squeak
And will-power?
Truth is
It is actually meek

I sneak coconut
Covered in
Yes
It's quite true
In Belgian chocolate
What can I do?
I found it by chance!

Well
That too is not exact
I hid it
In order not to protract
A kind of suffering that was sure to arise
When stuck with tofu, kale
Soup, stevia and rice
I hid it in order to be found by surprise
And confess it is pure pleasure
Beyond telling lies
To myself about chocolate wishes
Truth is
Nothing quite matches those happy swishes
As a two-pound Cadbury Milk Chocolate bar

It is like feasting great feelings
Straight from the jar
Reminds me of cigarettes I used to inhale

They beckoned
Made me run out the door
Feeling pale
Ran to the market
Yearning nicotine attack
Then resisted and bought a chocolate stack
Substituted Long Kent
For more delicious stuff
And never inhaled one other great puff

Saved those poor lungs to last to the date
When recycling this body
Would be up for debate
In the meantime, I plan to stay with that soup
And wait for signs of the final loop
Of life in this form
To do
You-know-what
That is all will say
Though the subject feels hot

Just remember that life is filled
With ups and with downs
No need to cover your goodness with frowns
Some good things are bad
And some bad things fantastic
So don't take measures that are too drastic

There is some pull in my bones
What is that strange calling?
Could that be Cadbury?

No more falling
From grace in your very own eyes
That for sure is your certain demise
Remember
Chocolate is good
Essential ingredient
On your journey through life
Its role is expedient

*****

GRIEF

May 5, 2013

Does grief ever go away?
Like, for example, pleasure diminishes
After you become accustomed to the object
Of its origin?
Does grief
Thin out over time?
Or does it get covered by the thickness
Of its unbearable intensity?
Like a blanket thrown over fire
Leaving a smoldering, blackened body
Or a corpse?

Did I dare to feel those piercing cuts
When suddenly my father was irreversibly gone?
Not lapsed into a coma
That could be a coma of hope
Or when a bubble in his lung collapsed him
Right in front of my eyes
While my mother's eyes refused to see
Long before what she feared most
Actually came to be?

Are we born with the knowledge of grief
Engraved in our cells
So that when it falls upon us
As we unsuspectingly wander through life
So that the very moment it falls upon us
It finds its nook
And settles right into the center of your heart?
And right from the center of your heart

Its soft wailing rises and swells
Until you will hear its call
Not the call that brings forth tears
Or heartache
Or stories of suffering
But that one inevitable call
To bring you home
To guide you
To the seat of your being

Trust me
There is no other location
To seek out
Grief **will** take you were you need to go
Grief **will** force your hand
And bend your knees
Until you find yourself in utter surrender
At the altar of the one Truth
That very Truth that held your grief
Held it safely
Until you followed its call
Found it waiting for you
Inside its nook
And in this single instant
You recognize
All you ever searched

*****

MEDITATION
May 10, 2013

There is only this moment
There is nowhere to go
There is nothing to think
That could change this moment
Or any other
There is no action to take
Other than the one that springs forth
From the very instant
In which it arises

*****

HANGING INSIDE
May 19, 2013

Hanging inside a decaying shell
Is not quite what I expected
I could not imagine
That living would turn
Into a battle
Quite as protracted
Did it ever occur to you
That life and death
Could be divided
By a wide long road of pains
No frills
And much of it unguided?

It seemed to me
That death just came
When youth was done and over
Well, maybe there was a thought
Or two
That middle-age could hover
Just slightly above final hours
Of decomposing woes
Just before
Well, so I have heard
You finally curl your toes

Curl them up
And show you are ready
To leave this body form
I really thought
Youth, age
Then death
Was more or less the norm

It is true
I witnessed young, close friends
And elders deconstruct
I even saw how some of them
Died long before life stopped
Yet still, it was not clear to me
That aging by itself
Without an illness or some cause
Could place you on the shelf
Of wild emotions
Flat on your back
Flat in the face of smiles
Stuck in the bottom
Of your old mind
Of long-forgotten guiles

So are you here
Still wondering
How come it is like this?
Did you not read the manual?
What else did you miss?
Have you been blind to everything?
Never took note of that
Which is so clear and obvious now?
Were you that lazy cat?
The one I mentioned previously
With body not bereft
The fact is
That you did not see
What was in store

A theft!

A theft of innocence
You manage to maintain

Until
One day
The moment here
To look and then reframe
The meaning of this life you live
The meaning of it all
The only thing that gives reprieve
When everything just falls
All things much less important now
Than what comes after death
So your pain gives way to bows
And attachments?
Less and less

Yet here you are
With some complaints
About this whole construction
Of how things work
In body form
Without proper instructions
Before you just deteriorate
And limp on to some temple
Or any house of prayer
Of sorts
Where words abound
Fears?
Ample

However what about this pain?
And that one?
And the heart?
A heart that beats relentlessly
To tell you, you are not so smart

Not smart enough to heed its call
To stop dead in your tracks
Allow a gentle rhythmic life
To slowly bring you back
And in its own words point the way
To what it stored inside
The jewel that lay there for you
Through this torrential ride
Of ups and downs
Through universes
And some strange adventures
Now you see
Here is the thing
It's when you take out your dentures
True readiness to die unfolds
The last part of this journey
Conclusion to this body trip?
Is travelling by gurney
But
There is no need to fear the final gurney
Once you remember that this journey
Though sometimes rather challenging
Does have mysterious offerings
Of sparks that point to the Divine
Sparks lighting up
Your flame and mine
When we are no longer you and me
And love is all we know and see

*****

NOT NOTHINGNESS

May 19, 2013

I have a question
Not the last one, I am sure
My question?
Is there a cure for losing trust
In what was formerly a must
In life?
Until that so auspicious moment
When joy just changes, turns to torment?
When gratitude becomes mere connotation
Of that which is your heart's salvation?
When your soul's music turns to noise
And meditation has no poise
Other than a body
Simply sitting?
Completely?
Like a thing
Omitting
Forgetting that you are not some lump
Of flesh and blood that tends to stomp
Around the universe
Or fashions stories
Or some verse

So where is your trust
When Nothingness emerges
And robs you of the best of urges?
And shrouds you in a cloudy fog
While you wish you were your dog
Your dog that doesn't have a clue
That there is something he might do

Other than eat, drink, walk and eat
Then eat again
It's no mean feat
To be contented
Even happy
While we start to feel quite scrappy
When Nothingness descends on us
So deep we do not even cuss

My question is
Do you absolutely trust
When subjected to life's thrusts?
Showing freedom in all conditions
To pierce
With sudden recognition
The veil of grey?
Unveil the sky no less?
With total glee, reveal a spaciousness
That has been yours
But you forgot
Until you saw that first blue dot
Of that which cannot ever end
It is your essence
It will send
You on a search forever
When one mere instant's ignorance
Just severed
Your awareness of what is true
It will guide you till you're blue

So now please just remember this
This Nothingness

Or deep abyss
Your pain,
Or illness
Or whatever
Are your doorways
Not a tether
To your suffering
Nor to losses
Nor to gains

Now take a look at what remains
When you look with naked eyes
And see the dance of subtle lies
Masking truth by sheer seduction
By all the layers of obstruction

Obstructions of the space inside
The very things that simply hide
Themselves within your naming
It is time
To stop this constant blaming
Of history or psychology
Just take one look
And you will see
That even in your darkest hour
There are no demons that devour
Other than your mind constructions
So drop those favourite concoctions
Some of the worst conditions
Beyond sad
Are exactly those that bring
With them the key ingredient

For waking up
Not all of them convenient

A prickling pain is what will drive
And push and coax and give you hives
Until it is clear to you that all
And everything is call
To take you home where you belong
That nothing can be possibly wrong
Even your very deepest pain
Will be vehicle to claim
True Nature
Inside the Nothingness

Astonishing this Truthfulness

*****

WHAT WE KNOW
May 19, 2013

Do you really know what's right?
Or wrong?
Or anything at all?
Other than not causing harm?
Or not following the call?
Do you really know, how life should unfold
And believe all the stories you have been told?

Do you really know what helping means
When you believe you hear a desperate scream?
A plea from a sick and suffering friend?
Do you know to show up and not try to end
The expression of that, which you believe is the cause
Of the Truth of their suffering with such force?

Do you really know a remedy that is certain?
Or might you become source of a thickened curtain
That will further obscure
Where the suffering is pointing?
I mean, have Compassion, without anointing
The suffering, as other than means to the end
Of what True Nature is choosing to send
Your way and help you wake up

Wake up from this dream and drink from the cup
That is offered
Unceasing
Unending
And bright

Now go
And dive through your suffering with might

With the might that only your heart can dispense
Then nothing can possibly be of offense
All doubts dispelled
All fears in the past
This is freedom
It is yours
At last

*****

A TEAR IN MY HEART
May 29, 2013, Train from Penn

I feel a tear in my heart
It makes me cry
It is familiar, but quite on the sly
I find it deepened, has stilled reactions
Nothing is left
But thought contraptions

There is a tear in my heart
I welcome its pain
It obliterates me
Yet something remains
It is all I have ever searched or desired
But have been blinded
And endlessly mired
In this and in that
In things and in matters
In opinions, words, concepts
Ran like a mad hatter
Solving problems with so-called solutions
Mixing cause and effect
Creating more confusion
Of what is quite real
And what's obviously not

Well, I almost completely forgot
All that I knew
Had suffered and learned
In those times when lessons had churned
Inside me
Demanding renewed attention

In a manner quite simply
Beyond comprehension
Demanding, insisting, persistently stern
Until I heeded the hot, raging burn
Of the tearing and ripping
Straight through my heart
The sadness and pain were only the start
Of a longing so great that ensued on their tail
It will pluck at your eyes and finally prevail

It forces to witness quite naked and true
And recognize all the original hues
Of Spacious Awareness
Always hiding right here
Inside the abode of your greatest fears

All it took was this tear in my very heart
For occlusions to swiftly and gently depart
As the focus of what we tend to call life
The life we all live
Filled with suffering and strife

So I tell you
Don't waste time and wait for the tear
Let go! Look inside
No need to stare
No need to strain, nor to force your gaze
You see?
I told you
You would be amazed

*****

FEAR OR EXCITEMENT
May 30, 2013, Whitestone Bridge, 12AM

Is this fear or excitement?
Is it pleasure or pain?
Is it hot or quite freezing?
Is this crazy?
Insane?

Do you know what you are feeling
When your heart starts to pound?
Do you know if you are excited
Or losing your ground?

I ask you
Have you ever thought
That your life was off track?
That your questions were growing
Yet the answers just slacked?
Slacked in meaning?
Turned rather trite
As your questions persisted
They just could not alight
Anywhere they directed
Their searchlight for truth
And brought back some memories
Of a time in your youth
When your questions were plenty
But answers were scarce
And your longing grew fiercely
While you could not disperse
The sweet whispers
That filled to the brim

Your heart and your being
Even when life looked dim?

And there wasn't a note
That quite matched what you heard
Yet you knew that the answer
Lay not in a word
Nor in writings
Nor teachings
Nor anything known
It had to emerge from your soul
On its own

On its own
Without compromise or other surrender
On its own
Even while the strands were so tender
That a push or a pull
Could just sever its weave
Yet your note just kept calling
Demanding to cleave
To its timber and pitch and make it heard
It wanted to fly
Soar
Just like a bird

A bird un-caged in jubilant flight
Isn't that what you felt
When you feared you just might
Lose your mind
Whilst it was liberating
Its waking urges

Exhilarating
Expressions
Manifesting the truth of your birth
All you need do is remember its worth
Not to you
But to everyone in your surrounding

Lead forth with your heart
With its truth resounding
Remember
It is up to you to give shape
To the formless expression
That wants to escape
From the soup of creation
Through the form that is you

Live and love with abandon
That is all you must do

*****

A SPARK

June 27, 2013, 2AM

There is a spark in me that lost its shine
There is a symphony from the Divine
I scan the universe to find the shards
Of what I know resides deep in my heart
But has been shattered by a wanton fate
A fate that came my way
And haunted me of late

A loss of that which I had found
The joyous fountain of the Unbound
It coursed through everything I ever knew
I recognized its sweetness
And then paid my dues
By leaping into it
Followed blind
The sirens' guiles
That beckoned heart and mind

A fall through drops of Truth
Onto cement
The grey and stony ground of fountains
Now
Completely spent
Those never-ending drops of pure delight
Which turn to bitter medicine
So bright
They sear your eyes, your soul
Your heart and more
And leave you searching for the exit door
From this existence that has taunted you

Yet right as you surrender
You notice sprinkled dew
In droplets on your wrinkled soul
Each one
Here to remind you
That you are whole
Each one a universe in its own right
Each one the same
But different with might
Of an intention fierce and undeterred
To live this life as fully as the bird
That pierces with its laser-like perception
Yet holds the view
That bears not one exception
Garuda-like
Stay on the path that's yours
Garuda-like
You simply will endure
Cement and fountain
You will see them both as one
It is all or nothing in this universe
Of fun
And pain and suffering and joy
For you to pierce the veil
And recognize the ploy

Wake up
Remember who you are
That sparkly drop of being
Yes
You are a star
You are heaven and earth

You are the moon and the sun
And you are
Tinkerbell
In woman and man

*****

NO GYROSCOPE
June 27, 2013

You have no gyroscope when you come into this world
There is no compass that guides you
When your life just swirls
My lover once told me these words and made me weep
He told me much more
And the truth was so deep
It resounded and echoed from down in my core
It ignited a song that pushed open a door
It felt like a calling from an ancient tune
Its reflection the truth of a mirroring moon

I remembered a time before questions arose
And all smells of this life were delight in my nose
I remembered a time, when each sound was like magic
And each note I could play was part of the fabric
Of everything known and still to be found
Of a fresh young life born on blood-soaked ground
Born to parents carrying unending pain
Born into history that tried to reframe
The experience of that which cannot ever be told
Tried to hide hearts that had simply
Turned
Cold
Had abandoned all of their basic humanity
Had hatefully steeped the world in calamity

Do you remember
When wonder transformed into fear?
Do you remember, when dissonance softly appeared?

I remember, when joy got covered by grey
And I stilled my voice
Could no longer relay
What I felt in their hearts and saw in their eyes
I covered the feelings that started to rise
From a place in my chest
That never gave rest
So I wheezed and coughed and thought it was best
To wait with the truth for some future date
Did you ever think it might be too late
To open the gate and let out the captives?

Your words and feelings of old
Held hostage
By the fears of a world that turned upside down
By the deafness of those who prefer to crown
Rather than look at what they know to be true
And quickly amend and correct what is due
What is required for hearts and nations to heal
But when a collective silence ensues and steals
Congruence, truth and the embrace of pain?
A pain so enormous, boundless
Beyond the remains
Of bodiless graves and heartless souls?
So this permeates endlessly into the holes
In the fabric
Of children's still forming impressions
Of how to be
In this world of endless transgressions

There is no gyroscope made for the ups and downs
For this endless symphony of human sounds

But deeply buried inside your heart
There lies a jewel that shines with a spark
So bright and pure is its musical sound
That it pierces the thickest walls in the ground
In the ground of your being
In the ground of all
And that is the compass that was installed
In your heart of hearts
In the core of your being
It is the gate to your inner seeing
When the world starts to crumble
And your balance is gone
Just remember your compass!
It resides in the dawn
Of that which is endless, nameless and sweet
It is all your mind has to ever keep
Remembering and knowing each second
Each day
Look inside
Without the slightest delay

Don't waste precious moments of your existence
Just follow your compass
With un-ending persistence
Follow your compass and cherish its grace
And never forget the Truth
Of your face

*****

ACKNOWLEDGEMENTS

In the process of writing this section, I found myself deeply moved, as the list of names grew into a seemingly never ending parade of all the cherished beings, who have enriched my life and thereby inspired the emergence of my Poetry Reflections. The subject matter of most of the poems mirrors the process of acknowledging all those who have either directly or indirectly, knowingly or unknowingly been instrumental in this publication. Since there simply cannot be one single cause for any situation or outcome, and this being my first book, I am writing this rather lengthy acknowledgement section with deepest gratitude and appreciation for all of you and for how so much love has blessed my life. The following acknowledgments are for those who have in some form or other supported or been involved in the MahnoDahno project and the subsequent publication of *Of Life And Other Such Matters*.

First and foremost, my fondest and most profound appreciation for my incredibly creative genius cinematographer, Bruce Petschek, whose love for poetry brought him into my life and has helped birth the MahnoDahno poetry-video series, who has happily listened to my poems hundreds of times and who has consistently encouraged their publication.

My gratitude for their unending interest and encouragement goes to my dear friends Ehud Amit-Cohen, Michele Cassou and Nancy Peterson, who over the span of four years - often way past midnight - attentively listened to and loved my spontaneous outpourings.

To my parallel huge-hearted mom, Shula Cohen, to my sweet

brother Harry and to my dear friend Adelchen Strauss with love and enormous appreciation for their support and for "seeing" and loving these poems long before I did and to Gloria Greenfield for enthusiastically supporting the video versions, insisting on their submittal to film festivals.

My gratitude to Rav Moshe Weinberger, Geshe Sonam and Rupert Spira, whose recognition of Truth in my poems continued to warm my heart and dispel lingering doubts.

With unending gratitude for the one and only Song Ahm for everything – known and unknown – and for his miraculous presence in my life.

My profoundest gratitude goes to Rick Ingrasci for magically opening the first doors, unveiling what I never dared believe, to Stan Grof for confirming it and cracking open a stubborn mind, to Dan Brown for pointing to the first flickers of recognition, to Thupten Kalsang Rinpoche for letting those flickers reveal to me the rider and the horse, to Adyashanti for bringing me home to the sweetest silence and to the laughter that continues to bubble from it, to Roger Castillo for thinking like an engineer, making everything so crystal clear, for his magical dominos and for his loving, generous feedback as to Truth reflected in my poems and the MahnoDahno videos and, of course, to Francis Lucille for taking no hostages in his utter precision and deeply caring Manjushri-like fierceness in expressing Truth and graciously exemplifying it and for his and Laura's most generous, warm welcome into their home, when life catapulted me their way.

Most special recognition for Craig, my favourite musician and the best Ex ever, for his astute vision and his sharp eye and ear, for his unceasing encouragement from the very beginning and for his relentless insistence to unveil

MahnoDahno and publish my video poems in written form.

With great admiration and love to the one-of-an-amazing-kind Shirley Zwang and to the other one-of-an-amazing-kind Lenny Swimms for holding my hand and sweetening my life with their unwavering love, support and encouragement.

With many thanks to the NYC Independent Film Festival for loving MahnoDahno and allowing him to emerge from the virtual realm into the real world and, of course, to my indomitable Yolusia Nash, who did the same by creating the poetry corner to feature my poetry on her weekly WABC Radio Show.

Very special thanks to my dear friends Dorit Harari, Schlomo Zach, Robin Casarjian, Rick & Doreen Leskowitz, David Margolis, DD, Judy Silverstein & Paul Hughes, Tom Alessi, Lynda Norman-Danzig, Jessica Schwartz, Fran Pechenick, George Perlman, Ruchi & Jonathan Bornstein, Jen Tawa, Tania MacNeil, Kayhan Civelek, John Matozzi, Karin Frey, Raj & Nita Thakur, Ellen & Glenn Prottas, Steven Teagarden and his angel wife Nicoletta, my cousin and friend Bracha Nattel, my niece-by-choice Jessie Peterson and my miraculous Leda Green for holding my hand in so many caring, sweet ways.

Profoundest appreciation for my wild soul-sister and "un-teacher" Michele Cassou for not only exemplifying, but also demanding true creative freedom, for Liz Anker for coaxing my voice out of hiding, to JR for magically unraveling the mysteries of what I could hear, but not identify by name, allowing me to pull out the music that has lived in my heart, for AP who, during her mysteriously short passage through the fabric of my life, loved MahnoDahno and relentlessly insisted that my poetry reflections should leave the confines of my notebook and go into the world.

Most heartfelt thanks to Cara More, Leya Reddy, Nabil Attia and to my soul-sister Marie Carmichael for showing up with the most spectacular generosity of heart imaginable.

Of course with much love and appreciation to my sister Julie and brother-in-law Anthony and with deep love and gratitude to my brother Harry and my sister-in-law Amy for being in my life and for their unconditional love and support throughout my frequent out-of-the-box adventures that led to this book.

My heartfelt thanks to my truly one-of-a-kind doctor Max Scheer, to Joseph Field, Tom Michaud, Bell & Yvonne & Lea & Tom Tam, Adel Kahil, Joan Cavalcante, David Cheng, Andrea Sorgato and my amazing friend Alex Marinkovic for appreciating MahnoDahno enough to patiently and lovingly patch me up after my endless all-nighters of making him come alive.

Greatest appreciation for Angelino Logiudice for faithfully keeping looming bureaucratic mayhem at bay and for my mother's devoted angel-team, Urszulka Pac, Elena Douglas, Josie Johnson, Gosia Krzeminska, Lorna Francisco, Maria Uczarczyk, Zofia Jodlowska, Caroline David, Ela Mieczkowska, Agnieszka Slack, Agnieszka Zaleska, Grace Kocyk, Elizabete Guedes and Justin Hirmes for giving me the peace of mind to write and create, knowing that my mother was always safe and sound.

And last, but certainly not least, with huge appreciation for my LogicPro genius, webmaster and friend Steve Catizone, without whom this book would never have seen the light of day, for his great ears, his versatile expertise and his wicked sense of humour, consistently cracking me up and unfailingly turning the tedious details of publishing, sound engineering and near-all-nighters into hilarious occasions.

ABOUT THE AUTHOR

BLAH BLAH BLAH BLAH BLAH BLAH BLAH
BLAH BLAH BLAH BLAH BLAH BLAH BLAH
BLAH BLAH BLAH BLAH

MAHNODAHNO & MAHNIDAHNI